Juan Carlos Jim

I0059517

The Significance
of Values
in an
Organization

Cograf Comunicaciones
August 2009

The Significance of Values in an Organization
First Edition in Spanish: November 2008
First Edition in English: August 2009

Copyright©2008 Juan Carlos Jimenez. All rights reserved.

Published by Cograf Comunicaciones (www.cograf.com)
Caracas - Venezuela.

Phone/Fax: (+58+212) 239-5864 / 237-9703 / 237-6630.
E-mail: libroscograf@cograf.com

The contents of this book may not be copied or transmitted either partially or totally, by any means, without the author's written authorization.

ISBN: 978-980-12-3779-2
Legal Deposit: if25220094282122
www.libroscograf.com

C O G R A F

When we listen carefully to conversations about values, we discover that people refer to them abstractly, as if they were not related to our daily actions.

It seems that we need to ask the following question more frequently: Are the values I verbally espouse in fact consistent with my behaviors and actions?

Experts on the subject have discovered that we need to pay close attention to this dichotomy, and achieve consistency between word and deed. Making values an integral part of our life requires as much dedication and persistence as going to the gym or caring for our health. However, for those who face the challenges and complexities of the contemporary workplace, it isn't obvious how to keep in shape with respect to values.

In this book, Juan Carlos offers key tools to surf through values. In simple language, with specific examples, he shows us a concrete way to strengthen values in organizations.

We will discover that values affect areas such as competitive strategies, innovation processes, creating new services for clients, work relations, and investment decisions.

As we shall see, all decisions reflect a set of values. Values drive decision-making. Combined with praxis and talent, values enable us to deliver value to our clients.

These pages provide ideas to ponder, but also exercises and actions we can implement immediately to affect our surroundings: the company where we work, the community where we live, or the family where we belong.

Juan Carlos provides a fresh approach to remind us of our endless capacity for self- improvement, adopting and disseminating positive values, and for transforming the ordinary into the extraordinary.

Cograf Comunicaciones
August 2009

Contens

1

An Introduction To Values

In this pocket book you will find practical references on the benefits that can be obtained when we reflect, individually and collectively, upon values. It is a text with educational purposes.

We can face the value crisis in organizations if we approach the subject in a practical manner, emphasizing the definition of actions, behaviors, and expected attitudes.

We must be aware that when we refer to values, our actions are much more important than what we think or say.

Our behavior reflects our values better than our thoughts. For example, if we say that all team members are important and valuable, we're contradicting our values if we disqualify the opinion of any of the members.

That person will feel devalued. His/her identity and commitment with the team will decrease. The other members will resent this, and the team will stop functioning.

For values to have more meaning in teams formed by people with common objectives, it is essential for members to share the explicit meaning of these values.

Our motivation is to help obtain a better understanding of organizational values, their purpose, and how to promote them in our daily activities.

An organization's values must be made explicit for all members:

- They must know them.
- They must agree with their meaning.
- They must understand the behaviors involved in expressing them.
- They must implement them.

If these simple conditions aren't met, an organization may end up professing very eloquent values in posters that look good on the wall, but have no clear, practical use for their members.

When the individuals in an organization "work" with the values that unite them, they achieve their objectives more efficiently and satisfactorily. They feel more united and motivated to be a part of the organization.

Working with values means making the necessary effort so that members of an organization agree on their practical meaning and implement them constantly.

But in order to work with values one must understand their importance (individually and collectively), their practical usefulness, the challenges they pose, and the way to promote them.

That's what this book is about. Make the best of it, and enjoy it.

2

The Importance Of Values

For humans, some things have always been more important than others. That is why we value people, ideas, activities and objects according to their significance in our life.

However, the criteria used to give value to those elements have varied throughout history, and depend on the values each person assumes.

Values allow the members of an organization to interact harmoniously. Values affect their formation and development as individuals, and make it easier to reach goals that would be impossible to achieve individually.

For the well-being of a community, it is necessary to have shared rules that guide the behavior of its members, otherwise the community will not function satisfactorily for the majority.

When families, schools, companies, and society in general function poorly, many times it is due to a lack of shared values, which is reflected in a lack of consistency between what is said and what is done.

For example, it is difficult to teach our children "tolerance" if our leaders and rulers constantly insult those with whom they disagree.

By the same token, it's difficult to promote "respect" if teachers, professors, bosses, or parents, when faced with complex situations, defend their decisions by saying, "Here you do what I say" or, "Things are like that because I say so".

In practical terms, a community is unlikely to function well, much less perfectly, if its members don't share certain principles that permanently guide the way they relate to each other, in good times and in bad times.

The word "community" means couples, families, the workplace, the classroom, the neighborhood, the city, the country, and any other place where people interact. If we don't share their values, we will neither feel at ease nor function properly in that community, and we'll feel little satisfaction in being a part of it.

In a company's organizational culture values are the foundation of employee attitudes, motivations and expectations. Values define their behavior.

If values don't have the same meaning for all employees, their daily work will be more difficult and cumbersome. The work environment becomes tense, people feel that they are not all moving in the same direction, and clients pay the consequences.

Being a pillar of a company, values not only need to be defined, they must also be maintained, promoted and disseminated. Only then will workers have a better chance of understanding and using them in their daily activities.

3

What Are Values For?

Values guide our behaviors; they are part of our identity as individuals, and guide our behaviors at home, at work, or any other area of our life.

They show us how to behave and how not to behave when we're faced with desires or impulses, whether we're alone or with others.

They are like a compass that helps us behave consistently, regardless of the situation.

For example, when using public transportation, some people give their seat to a pregnant woman, and others don't. The former believe in the value of courtesy and consideration towards others, whether they're strangers or not.

Among those who don't give up their seat we commonly find children (who haven't yet acquired that value), or elderly people who give a greater value to their own need to be seated (correctly so), or people who just attach a greater value to their own comfort.

Thus, values are the foundation of our behaviors, and make us feel well about our own decisions.

When we act guided by our values, we are not concerned by what others will say. We act according to our convictions, regardless of whether others are observing us or not.

When we truly believe that a set of behaviors constitute an essential cornerstone to life, we act accordingly, and don't care what others say about it.

When are committed to being honest, we don't take what isn't ours. We do so because we believe in respecting the property of others, not because we are being watched.

Values guide our actions and determine for us what's good or bad. When we're guided by values, we act without expecting anything in return, except personal satisfaction and fulfillment.

This satisfaction motivates us to espouse our principles and beliefs in all situations. It allows us to express a consistent personality, regardless of our mood or location.

Some people are not kind to others because they think they will receive nothing in return. Although they may be kind to the people they value (their children, students, employees or work mates), kindness per se is not a guiding principle in their life.

As parents, teachers, employers, or leaders, if we wish to foster certain principles and behaviors in others, we must practice those values consistently and through our behavior set an example.

– 4 –

WHEN ARE VALUES
USEFUL IN ORGANIZATIONS?

Values play an important role in the efficiency and effectiveness of organizations:

When they have the same meaning for all members of the organization (or at least for the majority).

» When they are shared and are equally important for all.

» When they are put into practice at all levels, particularly by leaders.

» When they are remembered every day.

Values in organizations help their members:

» Relate and function better, be better coordinated and better prepared in their planning, and achieve their goals efficiently.

» Be more aware of their direction and of the organization's short, medium and long term goals.

» Be collectively more creative and effective in meeting their challenges and fulfilling their tactical or strategic needs, both specific and general.

Consequently, the members of an organization with shared values:

» Feel more fulfilled as individuals and appreciate more their own behaviors.

» Feel very satisfied being part of that community, and feel more identified and committed to the purposes of the organization.

» Perform better, fulfill their specific responsibilities, and meet their professional commitments.

» Make more individual contributions and are more creative, because through their actions they feel more fulfilled and satisfied as individuals.

An organization's values are the pillars of its culture which, in turn, facilitates and assures the integration and growth of its members.

But the coherence of that culture, i.e. the degree of consistency between what its members say and do, is what determines the organization's level of harmony and performance.

As you can see, it is very beneficial for any organization to invest time and effort in fostering a culture based on shared values that are expressed through the everyday behavior of its members.

5

Some Challenges That Values Present To Us

First of all, values are intimately related to our emotions and feelings. For example, if we value honesty, then dishonesty disturbs us and hurts us. The same applies to sincerity, respect, responsibility or any other value.

We all occasionally have a hard time explaining our feelings. Similarly, in a community or in an organization, it's often difficult for us to agree on the practical meaning of a value.

This is due in part to the fact that each of us has our own hierarchy of beliefs, convictions and life principles.

We all build our own personal scale of values. Each of us acquires a set of values during childhood, and attributes significance to them according to our experience, knowledge, and development as individuals.

Furthermore, values can acquire varying significance depending on the position of the person implementing them.

For example, is publicly disclosing the identity of a person who has released private and confidential information justified in the name of "honesty"? It isn't easy to reach consensus on this issue. This generates controversy on the universality of some principles.

Values and their hierarchy can change over time. They emerge with a special meaning, and change throughout life, because they are related to individual interests and needs.

When we are children, our values are for the most part defined by subsistence and by wanting the approval of our parents. In our adolescence, our values are derived from the need to experiment and be independent, and when we are adults, we have other priorities.

This helps explain the obstacles we face in reaching agreements on the principles and beliefs of different people, in different moments in their life.

Lastly, values are closely related to morality and ethics. These are dense and complex philosophical concepts, and it is difficult to agree on their practical meaning.

It's for this reason that the meaning and usefulness of principles that help provide a sense of unity within an organization often become blurred.

When we make "a list of values" in organizations, we usually emphasize theoretical definitions. We can reach a general consensus on the ideas, but often lack practical expressions of the behaviors implicit in each value.

Our challenge is to translate these values into very specific behaviors in our daily life. In this way we will better nourish relationships between team members, and will achieve our objectives more easily.

If we translate values into concrete actions, they will acquire meaning and will be implemented in our families, our work, and in the organizations where we participate.

6

CRISIS OF VALUES

Although we are taught that honesty is a desirable, even ideal behavior (and we all accept this as true), the interpretation and meaning we give it in practice varies from one person to the other.

These differences are translated into very concrete attitudes and inconsistencies. For example, being honest, among other things, means to perform all our duties within an organization, but it is uncommon to associate being late with no justification with dishonesty.

Organizations tend to take for granted that all its members know what a value means, but its general definition is not enough for all to respond in the same way in situations with specific characteristics.

For example, a generalized consensus exists on the benefits of team work. It is an implicit value in an organization. However, it is also a behavior that gives rise to controversy. Team work doesn't happen automatically just because everybody is in the same place. Implementing this value in a harmonious manner requires special individual effort and courage. Therefore, great teams work and train a lot to achieve greatness.

What we call a crisis of values occurs when we find that our team members aren't following the organizational principles they're supposed to, or when they contradict those principles.

When we feel that we're not all going in the same direction great tension arises within an organization or community. This makes sense, because everything – reaching agreement, acting in a coordinated fashion, achieving established objectives -- becomes more difficult.

It is common in companies to talk about values such as excellence, leadership or innovation, but in most cases, the talk rarely goes beyond lip service or good intentions. The members of these organizations lack the guidance to understand the meaning of these concepts relative to the challenges they face in their daily lives.

Promoting excellence can be difficult in organizations that have arbitrary bosses, and innovation isn't easily assumed if arguments such as "why change if we have always done it this way and it works?" are frequently used.

These are only a few examples of the contradictions that produce the feeling that we have a crisis of values. When theory and practice are confronted, they generate stress, dissatisfaction, and crisis. In other words, it isn't easy to promote values if in our daily activities other principles or "anti-values" prevail.

These crises of values, beliefs, or principles occur when they start losing meaning and practical usefulness in concrete matters.

7

Why Are Values Weakened?

There are many reasons, but I want to highlight three that cause a sort of vicious circle in the deterioration of values.

1. Needs can be more pressing than values

Values themselves don't deteriorate. What weakens is our own capacity to believe in certain principles and their relevance, as a result of the pressure that certain needs exert on us. This in turn takes us back to the basic values of individual subsistence.

For example, when we decide we're not going to stand in line like everybody else it's because we consider that our individual needs are more important than those of others. With this type of personal belief, "honesty" loses meaning as a value that bonds us with a community.

This often happens in schools and similar organizations, when teachers or supervisors feel that their need to "control" the group has more value than the "respect" and "dignity" of its members, and use "authority" to impose order. They are surely going to have difficulty in obtaining "respect" in return.

2. It is much easier to convey other values

The real impact of values in an organization is reflected in the actions and attitudes of its members. It's our behavior that translates values into our daily activities:

Imagine a parent teaching her child the importance of truth or responsibility. A moment later, the child tells the parent that a debt collector has just called on the phone, and the parent casually says: "Tell him I'm not home."

Imagine something that happens frequently in a company: We don't look away from the computer while talking to a colleague we "respect", and saying something like: "I'm not looking at you, but I'm paying attention."

3. There is great social pressure in favor of "anti-values"

In a society that over-stimulates consumption, citizens end up being valued more for what they have than for what they are as individuals. As a result, appearance, or power often become higher values than responsibility, and we end up saying that "the end justifies the means."

When we talk about the formation of values, or when we demand them that certain values be adopted, we need to do so with a certain amount of humility. Values are reflected even in peoples' most casual behavior, and many of these behaviors are little more than habits, at times adopted unconsciously.

In this sense, values can be much more useful as a guide for the members of a work team or a family, when they are defined as leading to concrete, desirable behaviors.

8

A Definition Of Values

Values are principles that allow us to guide our behavior to fulfill ourselves as individuals. They are fundamental beliefs that help us prefer, accept and choose one thing over another or a behavior over another. They are also a source of satisfaction and fulfillment.

They provide a guideline to formulate goals and objectives, whether personal or collective. They reflect our keenest interests, feelings and convictions.

Values refer to human needs and represent ideals, dreams and aspirations. Their importance is independent of the circumstances. For example, even though we may be unfair, fairness still has a value. The same happens with wellbeing or happiness.

Values have worth in and of themselves. They are important for what they are, what they mean, and what they represent, and not for what others think of them. Values, attitudes, and behaviors are closely linked. When we talk about attitudes, we refer to the willingness to act in any given moment, according to our beliefs, feelings and values.

Values translate into thoughts, concepts or ideas, but what we appreciate most is behavior, what people do. Valuable persons live according to their values. Their worth is reflected in their values and how they express these values in their daily life.

Values also constitute the foundations for co-existence n a community and relations with others. They regulate our behavior to the benefit of collective wellbeing.

Maybe this is why we tend to relate to others using behavioral rules and norms, when in fact they are personal decisions. That is, we decide to act in a certain way and not in another, based on what value is important to us. We decide to believe in it and we value it.

When we enter an organization with already established values, we implicitly accept them and implement them. It's what others expect from us.

In an organization, values serve as a framework for the behavior of its members. These values are based on the nature of the organization (its purpose); why it was created (its objectives); and its projection into the future (its vision).

To this end, they must encourage the attitudes and actions required to achieve the organization's objectives.

In this regard, an organization's values should be reflected in the specific behaviors of its members, and not just in its mission statement.

If this isn't the case, then the organization should review the way it implements its values.

9

A Way To Define Values

The way values are defined in an organization can also be used to put them into practice. If they're only words and generic concepts, they're much less useful in practice than when they're defined in terms of attitudes, behaviors and specific actions.

This is because each of us, through our daily behavior, provides a particular value with a specific meaning.

For example, when an organization defines honesty as a value, it doesn't offer its members a clear guide to the specific behaviors implicit this value.

For example, one assume that members of a team will associate honesty with telling the truth and not stealing. However, it isn't common to associate honesty with offering all that we can deliver, with acting preventively, or with recognizing a mistake.

The organizations that benefit the most from applying values as a managerial tool translate them into codes of conduct, with precise indications regarding the attitudes and actions that favor the culture of the organization or community according to its interests.

Thus, values serve as a practical guide for the decisions we make every day at work. They help us identify what to do in each situation. Otherwise, the internal credibility of the organization, its leadership and its culture weaken, giving rise to a crisis of values.

Principles must be well differentiated from the objectives of the organization in order to be better understood as desirable behaviors. This confusion occurs frequently.

Values define objectives and point to the actions necessary to achieve them. Objectives can be flexible at a given point in time, but principles are immutable

Values should be like the columns supporting a building. Inside, we can make all the changes required, but we never move its foundations.

Leaders at all levels and areas of the organization are responsible for defining values. Heads of organizations, bosses, supervisors or coordinators, must be aware that everything they do or not do communicates the values of the organization to the rest of the team.

The other members of the organization are responsible for knowing the values of that community. If necessary, they must investigate and ask their immediate supervisors. The responsibility of understanding and implementing them is a value in and of itself.

We must remember that to define values, practice is more important than theory. What we do is more important than what we say, and this is valid for individuals as well as for organizations.

10

Using Values:
It's Your Decision

Although we begin to define our values at an early age, and each one of us attributes particular significance to specific values, how to put them into practice is a personal decision.

You decide what attitude and what behavior you'll assume in relationship to people, opportunities, difficulties or responsibilities, with varying levels of awareness. You decide to face them or avoid them.

When we want to establish a good relationship with other people, or want to be part of an organization, we decide to accept the values required for that relationship.

Even in an authoritarian organization, where values are imposed unilaterally, we also make the decision to accept them or not.

When we enter an organization or a community, we need to make an effort to get to know its values and their meaning. This allows us to regulate our behavior for the collective well-being, and to achieve a harmonious coexistence with others.

If we decide to be part of an organization with already established values, then we decided to accept them and implement them.

We can state that assuming the values of an organization we want to be a part of is an individual responsibility. The implementation of those values shows our degree of commitment to that organization.

Although this sounds simple enough, in fact it's difficult for organizations to get their members to share their values. In many cases this is rarely achieved.

Remember that when we speak of values, we mean principles and beliefs. So it is unlikely that we will follow something if we are not fully convinced of its importance or value. Can anyone force you to be convinced about it?

We can follow orders correctly, even if we don't agree with them. But using a value requires conviction, and this is your decision.

We all know that a job well done, backed by values, is superior to the one done just to follow an order.

You decide to implement your beliefs immediately. You decide not to postpone them. You decide to act according to your principles, from personal conviction, and not because you're being watched. You decide which attitudes are conducive to making you a member of an organization, and how you'll behave.

This capacity to decide is the source of your fulfillment as a human being.

11

Types Of Values

We can speak of universal values, because ever since human beings have lived in community, they have had to establish principles to guide their behavior towards others.

In this sense, honesty, responsibility, truth, solidarity, cooperation, tolerance, respect and peace, among others, are considered universal values.

However, in order to understand them better, it is useful to classify values according to the following criteria:

• Personal values:
These are considered essential principles on which we build our life and guide us to relate with other people. They are usually a blend of family values and social-cultural values, together with our own individual ones, according to our experiences.

• Family values:
These are valued in a family and iare considered either good or bad. These derive from the fundamental beliefs of the

parents, who use them to educate their children. They are the basic principles and guidelines of our initial behavior in society, and are conveyed through our behaviors in the family, from the simplest to the most complex.

• Social-cultural values:

These are the prevailing values of our society, which change with time, and either coincide or not with our family or personal values. They constitute a complex mix of different values, and at times they contradict one another, or pose a dilemma.

For example, if work isn't valued socially as a means of personal fulfillment, then the society is indirectly fostering "anti-values" like dishonesty, irresponsibility, or crime.

Another example of the dilemmas that social-cultural values may pose is when they promote the idea that "the end justifies the means". With this as a pretext, terrorists and arbitrary rulers justify violence, intolerance, and lies while claiming that their true goal is peace.

• Material values:

These values allow us to survive, and are related to our basic needs as human beings, such as food and clothing and protection from the environment. They are fundamental needs, part of the complex web that is created between personal, family and social-cultural values. If exaggerated, material values can be in contradiction with spiritual values.

• Spiritual values:

They refer to the importance we give to non-material aspects in our lives. They are part of our human needs and allow us to feel fulfilled. They add meaning and foundation to our life, as do religious beliefs.

• Moral values:

The attitudes and behaviors that a society considers essential for coexistence, order, and general well being.

12

ORGANIZATIONAL VALUES

Work has been a key element in the development of human beings, because it requires organization, planning, and effort.

Today, working and producing in coordination with others is an essential need, hence the emergence of organization in the work place.

Just as social life is framed within cultural values that allow for individual development, organizations also have their own culture. This culture must facilitate the integration and growth of its members, and its soundness is also proof of the soundness of the organization.

Organizational culture is the foundation of the identity and understanding of its members. It allows us to appreciate and organize the different situations that arise to respond to them in an appropriate and coherent manner. It provides the capacity to act in a strategic and efficient manner.

When we talk about culture in an organization, we refer to specific behavior patterns that can be recognized, conveyed and appropriated. It is the set of values used to organize the relations between its members.

The culture of an organization isn't present from the beginning; it is formed gradually, and is consolidated by the coherence and consistency between what its members say and do. This is an essential condition for the culture, to be conveyed to new members and to preserve its principles. But to convey a value, one must possess it and implement it; its credibility depends on it.

How an organization functions, well or poorly, is determined by the strength of its values. These function as an operating system which shows us how to meet our needs, and allows us to assign them a priority. They provide a common direction for all members, and establish guidelines for their daily commitments.

Values also inspire the purpose of each organization. The founders must be explicit about them from the beginning. In this way the value system of the company is best communicated, which in turn allows the existence of unified criteria that strengthen the interests of all.

The compatibility of personal values with organizational values leads to a high level of personal satisfaction with our work. The objectives of the organization and those of its members acquire greater meaning and importance.

If both of these values stray from each other, the culture of the organization weakens and its members begin to scatter.

On the other hand, organizations are subject to diverse dynamics and pressures, so its values are not formed once and for ever: they must be re-created, strengthened or modified as the organization evolves.

13

THE FORMATION OF VALUES

We start forming values in our childhood. First we learn to appreciate things that fulfill our basic needs, but we value especially those people that provide them to us. Their behavior towards us becomes the main reference of what is valuable.

Thus, our character and personality are molded through the attitudes and behavior of the people who raise us, whether they're our parents or other relatives. Their behaviors determine in large part what will subsequently become our most important beliefs and principles.

We learn to value the substance and the form of everything they say and do, and what they don't say and don't do. Each gesture or comment affects how we learn to make choices We also learn to differentiate between the theory and practice of values. The latter is what marks us the most.

So the consistency and coherence of our parents' behavior is what strengthens our formation. If they practice what they preach, our personality will be stronger than if they don't.

Later, when we are students, we start feeling social pressures and the pressure of values that are different from ours, as we relate to other people. The strength of the values formed through our parents is put to the test.

Values are often confused with habits, and many parents hope that school will form the values that were not instilled at home. This is not possible, because school does not fulfill the basic needs of life… that is the responsibility of those who raise us.

Teachers, leaders, and value models at school can reinforce what was formed at home, but they cannot replace them. If the convictions formed at home are not solid, they will soon be exposed to an intense social competition against other beliefs.

Why is it so difficult to form values? Because, unlike norms, values are convictions; they are behaviors we gladly decide to follow and produce satisfaction. We can follow norms against our will, but values have the support of our will. We have learned their importance due to the benefits they produce, individually and collectively.

Those who play a leadership role in our lives are most powerful at conveying to us their values. They are our parents, elder siblings, grandparents, some relatives, teachers, peers we admire, professors, and bosses.

However, to convey something, we must first possess it. Values are only conveyed through the example of our daily attitudes and behaviors. They can seldom be formed by explaining them or through a list of what is considered correct or incorrect. Memorizing their theoretical meaning does not guarantee their implementation.

14

FOSTERING VALUES
IN ORGANIZATIONS

In order for an organization to internalize a set of values its members must first identify with them. Management must assume the responsibility of defining, informing and cultivating them, according to the mission.

This is a two-way commitment. Leaders have the responsibility of promoting organizational values, and the rest of the members have the responsibility of getting to know them and implementing them.

The greatest challenge is not in the theory but in the practice.

Organizations foster values all the time, through the attitudes and behaviors of their leaders, at all levels. Every action conveys a value.

For example, if a company must give a course during a non-working day, it must properly communicate the reason for doing so. Otherwise, the organization ends up conveying the idea that continuing education is not work, and isn't very important.

Another example of a situation that conveys values contrary to those we wish to convey is when supervisors don't attend training sessions but rather send their subordinates, or when they do the opposite of what was taught in the course, or when they try to encourage effort or creativity with the argument that it "this is easy".

Promoting values like work, constant improvement, personal excellence, learning or proactive behaviors in organizations, requires courage and a special effort from leaders. What we do or don't do has a greater effect than words alone.

Those at the same level within an organization also communicate what their personal values are. For example, those who don't collaborate on a task end up losing the appreciation and respect of their peers.

In addition to defining them in terms of specific behaviors, organizations must show the practical benefits of implementing values. This is far from obvious to many. It's always best to make the outcomes explicit.

The most efficient way to foster values is to reinforce good practices and behaviors that better reflect the desired organizational culture. This is a proven and effective way to stimulate others to assume principles with conviction.

Threats and punishment in the best of cases produce only fear, not conviction.

The principle of positive reinforcement is simple: One cannot force people to do well what they don't want to do. This does not imply that mistakes must be overlooked or that we must be lenient. But positive reinforcement is much more than a pat in the back. For this method to work, people must receive praise immediately for a specific behavior, and we must express the positive feeling that implementing the value entails.

If this method is practiced systematically, the organizational environment works as a virtuous cycle of value reproduction.

15

Valuable People
In Organizations

In general, we value people for their principles, particularly for the attitudes and behaviors they show towards us. Of course, this process is a function of our own principles and beliefs.

However, there are values in organizations that have a generalized positive impact. Those who implement them are acknowledged, and held in high esteem. This is the basis of their capacity for leadership, along with their personality and their ability to affect the development of those around them.

People believe and trust them for what they are and what they do. Their behavior inspires admiration and respect. Their personality reflects a practice of values that inspires others within the organization to emulate them.

This happens with supervisors who are as attentive towards their work as towards the conditions of those under their supervision. It also happens with people who have such a sense of cooperation and solidarity that they're always willing to help others, even without being asked.

Sometimes such values are so absent in an organization that they'll cause as much mistrust as surprise.

An example is disinterested cooperation. People who do that attract the attention of even those who don't believe such a value exists in contemporary society, where material values prevail.

Something similar happens when we treat people with excellence. Aloof behavior, or feigned courtesy are so generalized in our culture that when we are treated with genuine respect and appreciation, we often don't know whether to be fascinated or suspicious.

The distortion of some values is such that many people have a hard time understanding how someone can give more than is "required" or more than what he is being paid for. Maybe this is because in a consumerist society we tend to give more weight to some material values than to others.

People who consistently practice certain behavior principles seem to be going against the flow and enter into conflict with established norms.

This happens with values such as creativity, innovation or striving to achieve. People with these beliefs also make a significant contribution for values to evolve or improve.

Of course, this will happen as long as the practical benefits of these "new values" are greater than those of the organization's "old values." Otherwise, there will be negative tension between those who practice one set of values and those who practice another.

In sum, valuable people in organizations are more proactive than the average members of their team.

They are not concerned about what others will say. They decide to practice their values with courage and respectful conviction.

They don't do it against all odds, but with all odds.

16

Ten Commandments
Of Organizational Values

The following are ten principles which, when followed, allow some organizations to perform at a higher level than others, and provide their members with greater personal satisfaction by belonging to them.

You can add, delete, or modify this list. It is just an exercise to show a way of presenting values more as behaviors than as theoretical concepts. In this way, they have greater practical meaning for the members of your team.

These came to me as I began thinking about organizations in general. Organizations subscribe to any number of values, and the particular behaviors related to these values can be described with more specificity. Think of it as a starting point to develop your own list.

Honesty:

We offer what we can deliver, and work hard to achieve it.

We act in an accurate and timely manner. We don't leave things to chance.

We honor and defend what belongs to others. We behave with integrity, consistently.

We are genuine in what we do. We have only one face.

We always act with justice in mind. We respect the truth.

We don't take advantage of the innocence or ignorance of others.

RESPONSIBILITY:

We accept responsibility for what we do or fail to do.

We make decisions with special care and attention.

We assume responsibility for our actions and their consequences.

Responsibility is an essential commitment towards others and ourselves.

We honor our debts.

We are well-prepared. We plan and make an effort to work in an orderly fashion.

We recognize our mistakes and strive to correct them.

COMMUNICATION:

We make an effort to listen to what others are trying to tell us. If we don't understand, we ask.

We try to make sure that we are explaining things correctly.

We don't take anything for granted. We don't make assumptions.

We avoid labeling our interlocutors or their messages.

We avoid prejudice.

We don't listen to gossip or rumors.

If we don't receive the information we need, we look it up.

We don't remain quiet when we have something to say.

We don't miss any opportunity for self-improvement.

SINCERITY:

We express ourselves freely, without dissembling.

We believe in truthfulness as the foundation for trust.

We say what we think, without harming others.

We act consistently with all people, and at all times.

We treat others with openness.

We believe in loyalty and transparency when we communicate.

Sincerity reflects appreciation for our teammates.

RESPECT:

We don't look down on others or their opinions.

We act with consideration and respect towards other peoples' feelings.

We appreciate those around us.

We make an effort to understand with empathy their points of view and the specific situations they are in.

We don't look down on people when we interact with them.

We don't insult or mistreat others.

We don't assault others either physically or verbally.

We treat people with dignity.

COMRADESHIP:

We create the success of our organization together.

Teamwork requires individual courage.

People who value this principle don't avoid being in a team with members with whom they have less in common.

The best result is achieved when everybody in the team does the best they can for themselves and for the group.

We don't achieve harmony by chance; it's the result of the effort of the people in an organization. It's based on knowing and appreciating all team members.

Solidarity:

We don't just help; we also commit to and share the situations of others.

We give support to another human being in need.

We understand that for solidarity to exist, two people or communities are required.

It means helping without receiving anything in exchange, even if no one finds out about it, without expecting reciprocity.

It means abiding by common principles and implies sharing benefits and risks.

TOLERANCE:

We respectfully accept opinions that are different from ours.

We don't discredit people who have points of view we don't share. We accept them with genuine respect for the individual, even though we don't see eye to eye.

Tolerance doesn't mean making concessions. It isn't indifference either.

It assumes that we know and accept the other person.

We choose to be tolerant because of our convictions.

It means understanding.

Tolerance implies willpower and maturity.

LEARNING:

We believe in constant improvement, learning from our everyday experiences.

We believe in the authority that knowledge, study and experience provide.

We therefore look for opportunities to update our knowledge, permanently and systematically.

We consider learning as a practical process of implementing behavioral change and adjustments, not just a way of expressing theoretical knowledge.

We say we learn after we have changed what was necessary to change.

Self improvement:

We are committed to improving what we do, every day, even if it's just a small part of the whole.

It's our ability and desire to overcome obstacles or difficulties. We're motivated by it.

Challenges inspire us.

We feel fulfilled as individuals when we make a conscious effort, because that's where we see our potential.

We don't do things half-way or because "it's my duty".

We believe in the power of discipline and perseverance.

17

An Idea To Work On Values

Develop and refine your organization's values with an open agenda. That is, draft a document that contains the behaviors and attitudes you want to see expressed by your group, with an example of how to implement each of the values of the organization.

It should be a document that can be updated and improved as the organization evolves, with the participation of its members.

In this way, you create the conditions necessary in order to "refresh" the practical meaning of those principles, and this will become an essential opportunity to strengthen commitment towards the values of the organization.

Creating a document with these characteristics also allows the creation of an essential identity so that values truly become the pillars of the organization's culture. In this way the members of the organization won't see values as just a simple list of beliefs they must adhere to, but rather a foundation which gives true meaning to being part of that organization.

Use the above mentioned universal organizational values as a starting point. With them, you can start creating a list of desired behaviors according to the different situations that the organization must face.

This is a down-to-earth way of associating the practice of values with the daily life of each member of the organization, while at the same time structuring a practical "code of conduct" that resonates with people.

Your document can be created based on the outline that is presented in the next page.

It's an example of how to outline a "code of conduct" that contains the meaning of values in terms of desired behaviors.

You can adapt it or formulate it differently, according to the requirements of your organization. However, the result must be the same: A practical guide for team members, who also participate in its creation.

Communication is fundamental.

If we face a situation where there's a lack of information about a project that's being executed, the attitude and behaviors of our organization's members should be the following:

1. Look for it. Ask.

2. Ask our peers and our bosses for help.

3. Don't speculate about why we don't have the information.

4. Don't start rumors.

5. Before judging, find out why there is a lack of information.

– 18 –

Final Comments

This list is just an example of how to create a "code of conduct" that contains the meaning of values in terms of desired behaviors. You can adapt it or make it differently, according to the requirements of your organization. However, the result must be the same: A practical guide for team members who also participate in its creation.

In the past two decades I've run hundreds of workshops helping different types of organizations define their values, and I have almost always encountered similar difficulties.

Many times "ethics" are considered a value, but ethics is a branch of philosophy that deals with morality, which is also considered a value. However, morality is formed by social conventions about what is good and bad, and has always been mired with contradictions. For example, political terrorists kill people to impose what they consider morally correct.

So with these types of references, values in organizations have become a source of controversy that in the end has few practical and useful implications.

Many organizations define their values as a sort of managerial obligation. They don't seem to be very clear or convinced about the benefits to their daily activities, or at least it isn't evident in practice.

This issue has become paramount to me in my work, because every action in every organization communicates values, and communications is my specialty.

It is very difficult to define and convey consistent, key messages for a company or product, if these messages are not based on the company's or product's values. Every act of communication act, in form and substance, teems with values.

Organizations transmit a message in everything they say and do, or in what they don't say and don't do. By the same token they also reflect the values of their mission and their public.

In this regard, it's of fundamental importance for every organization to understand and communicate the value of values.

I trust that I've made the point that organizations which have shared values can develop an organizational culture that allows them to perform with excellence, and in a manner far superior to those that don't share a consensus regarding their principles.

I also hope that this booklet will be useful to you in your daily professional life. And since I believe that communication, among other things, means having a constant two-way exchange, I would greatly appreciate your opinion of this booklet.

Please send your comments to my e-mail address: jucar@cograf.com.

Thank you for your time.

Juan Carlos Jiménez
August 2009

About the author

Juan Carlos Jiménez is a Venezuelan advertiser and entrepreneur. Since 1990 is CEO of Cograf Comunicaciones (www.cograf.com), but his proffesional expertise began in 1978 as a graphic designer.

He's dedicated to topics such as brand identity, graphic production, marketing, advertising, Internet projects, and customer care as a culture.

He is partner and founder of several active companies.

He has been invited professor of several Venezuelan universities on matters relating to corporative image and web marketing. And he has been a lecturer on national and international events.

Author of followings books: "Negocios.com" ("Business.com"), 2000; and "Mercadeo.com" ("Marketing.com"), 2006, and "E-mail at the workplace".

He has also published other works in the same format of this book: "The supreme art of customer service", "Take good care of me", and "Enjoy teamwork".

He's designer and facilitator of workshops on strategic planning, corporate communications, creativity, teamwork, change management and promoting values inside organizations.

E-mail: jucar@cograf.com
Twitter: jucarjim

Other book by Cograf Comunicaciones:

E-mail at the workplace
A Survival Guide. Solutions and Tips.
Author: Juan Carlos Jiménez

At Amazon.com:
• Paperback Edition: http://bit.ly/ve0Ug
• Kindle Edition: http://bit.ly/8sU4y

"For a corporate leader trying to make profit goals, for an entrepreneur trying to get an edge, for a manager trying to manage better or a staffer looking for more time in his or her day, I'd say that your book is nothing less than essential reading".
Robert Duncan. President, Duncan/Channon, Inc., San Francisco, California.

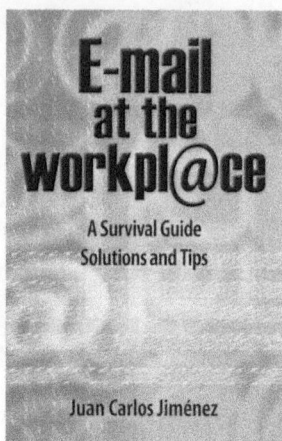

"Read this book! It's a must. It's like a grammar book for e-mails. Keep this book with you and refer to it when you feel you need it. I like it because, like a grammar school book, chapters are short and you can easily find the solution you are looking for."
Michel Goddet, Managing Director, IN-Advertising.com, Paris.

"After reading this book, I am shocked. I find that that email not only influences the recipient - it also defines the sender's personal image. And that includes corporate image. Juan Carlos takes us on a journey, rediscovering and exploring the world of the email."
Fumihiko Iwamoto, CEO, K&L Advertising, Hong Kong.

"When I was reading your book I have discovered several surprises about the obvious, which are important to me as a manager and as an owner of the company. The first one is the cost of an e-mail. I thought is for free, and you tell me there are costs associated."
Krzysztof Przybylowski, CEO, CAM Media, Warszawa, Poland.

"This book gives us the power to understand its realities and the ability to reclaim the time and space that email occupies and to reshape our engagement with this techno-sociological phenomenon. What's more, it contains the kinds of guidelines that would make the world of email truly civilized."
Eric Mower, Chairman/CEO, Eric Mower and Associates, New York.

"This is a profound, simple and practical guide; a timely, necessary and very fortunate publication. It delivers the power of simplicity, and must be part of the managerial toolbox of successful businessmen that are flexible, and open to change."
Italo Pizzolante, CEO, Pizzolante Comunicación Estratégica, Venezuela.

"Your book helps create a path through the haze -a simple, direct and cleverly constructed roadmap back to order that will help save time, money and life. The learnings from this book will certainly help my business."
Craig Poole, Managing Director, Synchromesh Marketing & Creative Communications, Sydney.

If you want to make a present of this book
to co-workers, colleagues, family and friends,
please, write me to jucar@cograf.com.
I can offer you a better price for volume.

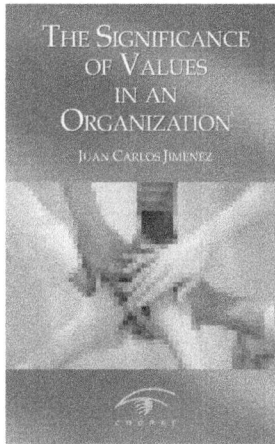

THE SIGNIFICANCE
OF VALUES
IN AN
ORGANIZATION

JUAN CARLOS JIMENEZ

Other books by Cograf Comunicaciones:
www.libroscograf.com

Cograf Comunicaciones
www.cograf.com

www.ingramcontent.com/pod-product-compliance
Lightning Source LLC
Chambersburg PA
CBHW032016190326
41520CB00007B/503